# North Country Cooking

by

Dorothy and Bob Igoe

NORTH COUNTRY COOKING

ISBN 0-925168-46-7


Library of Congress Cataloging-in-Publication Data

In Progress

*Cover:* Great Sacandaga Lake, c. 1938

North Country Books, Inc.
311 Turner Street
Utica, New York 13501

# Foreword

*North Country Cooking* is an outgrowth of a small book Dorothy edited about six years ago. That volume got its inspiration from Dorothy's grandmother's (Julia Pattengill) personal handwritten collection of recipes which she had entered from about 1870 to the early 1900's. Tucked in the pages of that book were many clippings of household hints and home remedies from such diverse sources as *The New York Times*; *Rural New Yorker*; *The Farmer's Almanac*; *The Milk Can*; *Watkins' Almanac*; *Home Doctor and Cookbook* and several country newspapers. These hints and a few more are included in this volume.

The idea of this cookbook is to present over 100 recipes, many old fashioned ones, that are comparatively easy to make using ingredients that are not too difficult to find. Included are recipes which might be used in the North Country, using ingredients native to the area.

We want to thank friends who gave us recipes. Many come from Dorothy's files and we can't identify the original source. I recently found the recipe for "Never Fail Chocolate Cake" that I used at the I-Go-Inn some fifty-seven years ago. This and many other old favorites appear in this collection.

—*Robert Igoe, Sr.*

# Acknowledgments

We want to thank our many friends and relatives who we used as guinea pigs to test various recipes that we've included in this book.

And thank you to the following people who have shared some of their favorite recipes for us to enjoy.

Helen Bryden, Mike Condon, Sharon Condon, Kristen Crain, Carroll-Brennan-Foelix, Ann Gregory, Martha Gulley, Jerry Harper, Betty Heilig, Ellen Hemink, Peggy Igoe, Lynn Igoe, Betty Matteson, Sally Myhr, Marie McGrath, Sheila Orlin, Shirley Powers, Trudy Pfrimmer and Ellie Wilgus.

Special thanks to Eleanor and Hersey Trombly of Chazy, New York for recipes submitted by their daughter, Rhonda Daley. These are really North Country cooking —you can't get much farther north in New York State— and include dishes made with maple syrup, blueberries, blackberries and butternuts.

Thanks also to Audrey Sherman for typesetting, Sheila Orlin for editing and Rob Igoe, Jr. who I hope will sell a lot of this book.

# STARTERS

# Cheese Popovers

1 cup water
1 tsp. salt
¼ tsp. pepper
¼ tsp. nutmeg
5 Tbs. butter or margarine
1 cup flour
1 cup Swiss cheese, grated
5 large eggs

*Makes about 35—Preheat oven to 425°*

In saucepan bring water, salt, pepper, nutmeg to a boil; add butter. When butter has melted remove from heat. Add flour and beat with wooden spoon until mixture leaves side of pan. Add cheese and beat thoroughly. Beat in four eggs, one at a time until mixture is smooth and firm. Drop from teaspoon on greased or non-stick cookie sheet. Beat remaining egg with ½ Tbs. water and brush top of puffs with mixture. Bake in preheated oven for about 20 minutes or until golden brown. Serve immediately.

*When sweeper brush bristles become soft from long use and do not sweep up lint as well as when stiff, put a little common baking soda in some hot water; take the brush out of sweeper and dip it up and down in this. Let it dry in the sun and it will be like new. Hair brushes or any brush can be treated in the same way with the best of results.—c. 1900*

# Sausage Balls

12 oz. cheddar cheese
1 pkg. frozen loose sausage, thawed
2 cups Bisquick

*Preheat oven to 450°*

Melt cheese in double boiler. Brown sausage and drain. Mix Bisquick, sausage and cheese together and form into ¾-inch balls. Bake on cookie sheet at 450° for 8 to 10 minutes.

# Cocktail Franks

1 cup currant jelly
½ cup mustard
2 pkgs miniature hot dogs

*Preheat oven to 350°*

Mix jelly and mustard together in small casserole dish. Add cocktail franks and stir. Bake at 350° for 30 minutes. Serve piping hot on toothpicks.

# Stuffed Mushrooms

1 pkg. fresh mushrooms
½ lb. country style sausage
½ lb. mozzarella cheese, shredded
¼ cup Italian style bread crumbs

*Preheat oven to 450°*

Clean mushrooms, chop stems and put caps aside. Brown the sausage, adding the chopped mushroom stems and saute for a few minutes; drain. In a separate bowl mix cheese and bread crumbs; add sausage and mushroom stems. Put mixture inside mushroom caps. Bake at 450° for 10 to 15 minutes or until mushrooms are brown.

# Hot Dip

8 oz. pkg. cream cheese
1 cup sour cream
2 oz. chipped beef, shredded
2 Tbs. milk
2 Tbs. green pepper, finely chopped
1 Tbs. onion flakes

*Preheat oven to 350°*

Mix all ingredients well. Bake at 350° for 20 minutes. Serve with assorted crackers or bread.

# Spinach Squares

4 Tbs. margarine
3 eggs
1 cup milk
1 cup flour
½ tsp. salt
½ tsp. baking powder
12 oz. Monterey Jack or cheddar cheese, grated
¼ cup onions, chopped
2 pkgs. chopped spinach, thawed and drained

*Preheat oven to 350°*

Melt margarine and pour into 9 x 17" baking pan. Beat eggs, add milk, flour, salt and baking powder. Mix well and stir in cheese, onions and spinach. Spoon into greased baking pan. (If using a heat resistant pan, lower heat to 325°.) Bake 35 minutes. Remove from oven, let set about 15-20 minutes, then cut into 1" squares for hors d'ouvres or larger for main dish.

*Powdered alum scattered on shelves will drive away ants.*
*—1889*

# Shrimp Dip

8 oz. pkg. cream cheese
1 can cream of shrimp soup
1 tsp. lemon juice
¼ tsp. garlic salt
dash of paprika
1 can tiny shrimp, drained

Soften the cheese at room temperature. Mix together with soup, juice, salt and paprika. Stir in shrimp. If you like it spicier, add some horseradish. Serve with potato chips.

# Hot Artichoke Dip

2 cans artichokes, drained and chopped
2 cups mayonnaise
2 cups grated Parmesan cheese

*Preheat oven to 350°*

Mix above ingredients. Bake in casserole dish at 350° for 15-20 minutes until bubbly. Serve with assorted crackers.

# Mushroom Meatballs

1 can cream of mushroom soup
1 lb. ground beef
½ cup fine dry bread crumbs
2 Tbs. onion, minced
1 Tbs. parsley, minced
1 egg, slightly beaten
1 Tbs. bacon fat or oil

*Serves 4*
*So good you may want to double or triple this recipe*

Measure out ¼ cup soup. Combine with beef, bread crumbs, onion, parsley and egg. Shape into 16 meatballs about 1½ inches in diameter. Brown in fat in skillet. Blend remaining soup with water (can use ½ cup beef bouillon instead); pour over meatballs. Cook over low heat about 10 to 20 minutes, stirring occasionally. Excellent served with noodles or meatballs. Can be made smaller and served as hors d'oeuvres.

*Keep unpopped popcorn in your refrigerator until ready to prepare—you'll find fewer unpopped kernels resulting.*

# Dorothy's Cheese Puffs

1 loaf white bread, unsliced
1 cup margarine
8 oz. pkg. cream cheese
1 lb. cheddar cheese, grated
4 egg whites, stiffly beaten

*Preheat oven to 350°*

Cut bread into 1" slices; then cut each slice into 9 pieces. Melt margarine and cream cheese in double boiler. Add grated cheese. Beat until smooth. Fold in stiffly beaten egg whites. Dip bread cubes in mixture to coat, then place on cookie sheet. Refrigerate until set. Lift from cookie sheet and put in plastic bag. When ready to use, place on ungreased cookie sheet about 2" apart and bake at 350° for 8 to 10 minutes or until lightly browned. Can be prepared ahead of time and frozen to bake later.

# Ham Roll-Ups

1 bunch green onions
8 oz. pkg. cream cheese, softened
1 pkg. sliced ham, rectangular shape

Clean and trim onions to length of ham slices. Spread ham slices with cream cheese. Place one onion on each slice and roll up. Slice rolls into ½" pieces, forming pin-wheel. Refrigerate until ready to serve.

# Stuffed Cherry Tomatoes

15-20 cherry tomatoes
½ lb. bacon, cooked and crumbled
½ cup mayonnaise
¼ cup green onions, chopped
2 - 3 Tbs. grated Parmesan cheese
2 Tbs. fresh parsley, finely chopped

Cut tops off tomatoes, scoop out pulp and discard. Drain tomatoes. Combine remaining ingredients and mix well. Put mixture in tomatoes and refrigerate for several hours.

*To hasten the ripening of garden tomatoes, put them in a brown paper bag, close the bag and leave at room temperature for a few days.*

# SOUPS &
# STEWS

# Squash Soup

1 cup cooked squash
1 qt. milk
2 slices onion
2 Tbs. butter or margarine
3 Tbs. flour
pinch of celery salt
pinch of pepper
1 tsp. salt

Put squash through sieve before measuring. Scald milk with onion. Add milk to squash, discarding onion. Cook butter and flour together and add to soup. Add spices to taste and serve in warmed bowls.

# Parsnip Chowder

1 qt. milk
6 soda crackers
¼ lb. salt pork, diced in small pieces, crisply fried
1 onion, chopped
2 cups parsnips, cubed
2 cups potatoes, cubed
2 cups boiling water
salt and pepper to taste

Pour milk over broken crackers and set aside. In small amount of drippings from salt pork, add onion and cook slowly. Add parsnips and potatoes, cook until lightly browned. Add boiling water, salt, pepper and salt pork. Cook until vegetables are tender. Add crackers to chowder and reheat. Serve in heated bowls and garnish with chopped parsley if desired.

# Corn Chowder

4 medium onions, coarsely chopped
2 Tbs. butter or margarine
4 medium sized potatoes, cubed
1 qt. milk
½ cup light cream
½ stick butter or margarine
32 oz. canned creamed corn
1½ tsp. salt
¼ tsp. pepper
pinch or two of thyme
¼ tsp. parsley flakes

*Serves 6 to 8*

Fry onions in butter until brown. Simmer cubed potatoes for 15 minutes; drain. Warm milk, cream and ½ stick butter in large pan, add rest of ingredients. Heat until piping hot—do not boil—stirring frequently. Set aside to cool. Reheat before serving. Good with a little pepper sprinkled on top.

*Black stockings should be rinsed in blue water to give them a good color.*—c. 1900

# Hearty Venison Soup

1½ lbs. venison, cut into ¾" cubes
Italian dressing
¼ cup vegetable oil
2 tsp. salt
½ tsp. pepper
4 cloves garlic, thinly sliced
¼ tsp. onion powder
2 qts. water
3 beef bouillon cubes
4 stalks celery, coarsely chopped
4 small onions, halved
4 medium potatoes, quartered
1 green pepper, coarsely chopped

*Serves 6 - 8*

Marinate venison in Italian dressing for 4 to 5 hours in the re-frigerator. In a heavy skillet, add oil, salt, pepper, garlic, onion powder, and venison and saute until brown. In a separate pot bring 2 quarts water to boil, add bouillon, celery, onions, pota-toes, green peppers and venison mixture (do not drain). Simmer approximately one hour or until vegetables are tender.

*When poaching eggs, a couple teaspoons of vinegar added to the boiling water will help the eggs hold their shape.*

# Strawberry Soup

1 qt. strawberries, cleaned and hulled
¾ cup dry white wine
1 cup sour cream
¼ - ½ cup sugar
4 cups cold water

Blend the first four ingredients until smooth. Add the water to the above and mix with rotary beater until well blended. Transfer mixture to saucepan and heat slowly. Do not boil. May be served hot or cold.

# Chestnut Soup

15 oz. can chestnut purée, unsweetened
3 cups water
1 medium onion, finely minced
2½ Tbs. butter
¼ tsp. white pepper
4 chicken bouillon cubes, dissolved in
1 cup boiling water and cooled
1 tsp. sugar
1 cup heavy cream, scalded

*Serves 6*

Combine purée and water in large saucepan. Blend until smooth. Add onion, butter, pepper, bouillon and sugar. Bring to a boil, reduce heat and simmer gently for 20 minutes. Add cream, stirring constantly. Heat thoroughly, but do not boil.

# Bean Soup

2 cups dried beans, shelled
6 cups water
1 ham bone or 1½ lb. ham butt
½ cup onion, chopped
1 cup celery with leaves, chopped
1 qt. canned tomatoes
¾ cup potatoes, diced
1 tsp. salt
¼ tsp. pepper

*An old fashioned recipe that will serve 10*

Wash beans, add 6 cups water and boil for 2 minutes. Remove from heat and let stand for 1 hour. Simmer beans without draining until tender, about 2 hours, adding more water if necessary. In meantime simmer ham in water to cover. Skim fat from ham broth and add tender beans. Stir in remaining ingredients and simmer until potatoes are tender, about 20 minutes. A small amount of grated horseradish can be added to liven the flavor.

*One part of turpentine to three parts of linseed oil makes the best piano polish one can find. Good also for hardwood floors.*

# Spicy Potato Soup

1 lb. ground beef
2 Tbs. vegetable oil
4 cups potatoes, peeled and cut into ½" cubes
1 small onion, chopped
24 oz. canned tomato sauce
4 cups water
2 tsp. salt
1 tsp. pepper
¼ to ½ tsp. hot pepper sauce

*Serves 6 to 8*

In a large Dutch oven or large kettle, brown ground beef in vegetable oil and drain. Add potatoes, onion and tomato sauce. Stir in water, salt, pepper and hot pepper sauce. Bring to a boil, lower heat and simmer for 1 hour or until potatoes are tender and soup thickened.

*Chamois is one of the few things which come out smooth and soft from washing if wrung directly from the soap suds without rinsing in clear water. The latter process tends to harden it.*

# Venison Stew

2 lbs. venison, cut into 1" cubes
meat tenderizer
3-4 slices bacon
3 cups water
1 tsp. Worcestershire sauce
1 tsp. garlic powder
½ cup onion, chopped
1½ tsp. salt
¼ tsp. pepper
4 medium potatoes, cut into 1" cubes
6 carrots, sliced
2 cups celery, diced
4-6 small onions, halved
¼ cup water
2 Tbs. flour

*Serves 6 -8*

Tenderize venison with tenderizer according to instructions. Cook bacon, then brown venison in bacon fat in large Dutch oven. Add 3 cups water, Worcestershire sauce, garlic powder, chopped onions, salt and pepper. Cover and simmer 2 hours. Add potatoes, carrots, celery and onion halves. Cook until vegetables are tender (15-20 minutes). If gravy needs thickening, make a paste mixing ¼ cup cold water with 2 Tbs. flour and add to the stew.

# Pork and Beer Stew

2 lbs. boneless pork, cut into 1" pieces
¼ cup flour
salt and pepper to taste
2 Tbs. oil
2-3 onions, sliced
¼ tsp. thyme
12 oz. can of beer
parsley, stems and leaves
small bay leaf
1½ cups carrots, cut into 2" pieces

*Serves 4*

Coat pork with flour, salt and pepper. Heat oil in stew pot, brown pork pieces. Add onions and toss until glazed. Add thyme and beer. Tie parsley stems and bay leaf together to make a bouquet; add to pot. Cover and simmer until meat is almost tender and sauce is browned, about 1½ hours. Add carrot and cook until tender. Remove herb bouquet. Garnish with chopped parsley leaves and serve with caraway noodles or boiled new potatoes.

*Oilcloths will last longer if one or two layers of wadded carpet lining are laid under them.—1889*

# SALADS

# Hot German Potato Salad

6 medium potatoes (2 lbs.)
¼ lb. bacon, diced
2 Tbs. onion, finely chopped
¼ cup beef bouillon
¼ cup vinegar
1 tsp. salt
2 tsp. sugar
¼ tsp. pepper
1 Tbs. parsley, finely chopped

*Serves 4 to 6*

Boil potatoes in skins until fork tender; peel and slice while hot; keep warm. Fry bacon until golden; add onion and stir while cooking. Do not drain. Add bouillon, vinegar, salt, sugar and pepper to bacon mixture; heat to boiling. Pour over hot sliced potatoes; toss gently. Serve warm or hot. Garnish with parsley.

# Cranberry Salad

3 oz. pkg. cherry Jello gelatin
1 cup boiling water
1 can whole cranberry sauce
1 can mandarin oranges, drained
½ cup sour cream
¼ cup walnuts, chopped

Make cherry gelatin with boiling water. Mix in rest of ingredients, pour into gelatin mold and refrigerate to set. Serve on a platter garnished with lettuce and fresh cranberries.

# Marinated Vegetable Salad

4 cups fresh cauliflower florets
2 medium zucchini, sliced into ¼" slices
boiling water
1 pt. cherry tomatoes

In large saucepan blanch cauliflower and zucchini in boiling water for 1 minute; drain. Prick holes in cherry tomatoes. Add dressing below.

## Dressing

½ cup salad oil
¼ cup olive oil
¼ cup white wine vinegar
1 Tbs. parsley, minced
1 Tbs. onion, grated
2 tsp. salt
¾ tsp. dry mustard
½ tsp. chervil

Combine above ingredients and mix well. Pour over vegetables and stir until coated. Refrigerate 3-4 hours or overnight, stirring occasionally. Spoon vegetables out with slotted spoon. Serve in a bowl and garnish with lettuce.

*Polish your stove with old newspapers.*—1889

# Lemon Jello Mold

3 oz. pkg. lemon Jello gelatin
1¼ cups boiling water
¾ cup sour cream
¼ cup mayonnaise
1 Tbs. sugar
1½ tsp. fresh lemon juice
1½ cups apples, peeled and coarsely chopped
1½ cups seedless grapes, halved
½ cup pecans or walnuts, chopped

Dissolve gelatin in boiling water, cool slightly. Combine other ingredients, add to gelatin. Pour into pan or mold and chill until firm.

# Raspberry Jello Mold

6 oz. pkg. raspberry Jello gelatin
1 small can crushed pineapple
1 pkg. frozen raspberries, thawed
½ - 1 cup walnut pieces
2 cups sour cream

Prepare gelatin using ¼ less water than called for. Drain fruit well, add to gelatin and add nuts. Pour about ½ mixture into mold, chill until firm. Spread sour cream on top of chilled gelatin and pour remaining gelatin on top of that and chill until firm. Serve garnished with lettuce and fresh raspberries.

# Hot Chicken Salad

4 cups cold cooked chicken, diced
2 Tbs. lemon juice
¾ cup mayonnaise
2 cups celery, chopped
4 hard boiled eggs, sliced
½ tsp. Accent
¾ cup cream of chicken soup
1 tsp. onion, chopped
1 small jar pimentos
1 cup cheddar cheese, grated
1½ cups potato chips, crushed

*Serves 6*

Combine first nine ingredients and stir. Place in refrigerator overnight. Before serving, top with cheese and potato chips Bake at 350° for 35-45 minutes.

# Beet Salad

1 medium can sliced beets
½ cup sour cream
¼ cup horseradish
1 tsp. sugar
salt and pepper

Drain beets and cut into julienne strips. In a separate bowl mix rest of ingredients and pour over beets. Mix well. Serve on greens; garnish with chives.

# Carrots with Dill Dressing

15 medium carrots, cooked and thinly sliced
½ medium onion, chopped
½ tsp. dill
¼ tsp. pepper
½ tsp. sugar
¾ tsp. salt
2 Tbs. corn oil
1 Tbs. wine vinegar

*Serves 6*

Mix all ingredients together and served chilled.

# Bleu Cheese Dressing

1 qt. mayonnaise
8 oz. pkg. bleu cheese, crumbled
½ cup light cream
1 tsp. horseradish
1 tsp. vinegar
¼ tsp. each salt, pepper, garlic salt

*From the former Maxwell House Restaurant in Utica, NY*

Mix all ingredients thoroughly. Makes one quart plus another half pint.

# Layered Salad

1 head crisp iceberg lettuce
8-10 stalks celery, cut in small pieces
2 green peppers, cut in ½" pieces
1 large sweet onion, thinly sliced
10 oz. pkg. frozen peas, cooked and drained

Layer ingredients in a large glass bowl in order given, reserving half of lettuce for top. Add dressing below.

## Dressing

1 cup sour cream
1 cup mayonnaise
2 Tbs. sugar
1 cup cheddar cheese, grated

Mix sour cream and mayonnaise and carefully spread over top of salad (don't mix). Sprinkle sugar and cheese over the top. cover bowl with plastic wrap. Can be refrigerated for up to 24 hours.

*Add a can of sliced beets to leftover pickle juice. Let stand overnight and you'll have delicious pickled beets.*

# Chick Pea Salad

1 clove garlic, crushed
¾ tsp. oregano
4 Tbs. sweet onion, minced
1 tsp. basil
½ tsp. salt
½ tsp. pepper
2 Tbs. wine vinegar
½ cup olive oil
2 tsp. Dijon mustard
2 20-oz. cans chick peas
¼ cup mayonnaise
2 Tbs. parsley, chopped
3 Tbs. scallions, chopped

Mix first nine ingredients. Heat peas until boiling, drain and mix at once with ingredients and cool. Before serving, toss with mayonnaise, parsley and scallions.

*Kerosene will take iron rust and fruit stains from almost every kind of goods, without injuring the fabric. Wash the soiled spot in kerosene as you would in water. The spots must be washed in the kerosene before they have been put into soap and water, or it will do no good.*—c. 1900

# Fruit Salad

2 green apples, chopped
2 red apples, chopped
1 cup each green and red grapes, halved
2 stalks celery, chopped
2 cans mandarin oranges
½ cup walnuts, chopped

## Dressing for Fruit Salad

1 cup sour cream
¼ cup mayonnaise
2 tsp. sugar
¾ tsp. grated orange or lemon peel

Combine all ingredients for salad. Mix dressing and pour over salad.

*When whipping egg whites, add a pinch of salt to make them fluffier. And for extra-high meringue, add a small amount of baking powder.*

# MAIN COURSES

# Chicken and Dumplings

3½-4 lb. chicken, cut up
½ cup flour
1 tsp. salt
½ tsp. pepper
2 tsp. vegetable oil
4 medium onions, quartered
2 tsp. garlic, minced
4-5 carrots, cut into 1" pieces
2 parsnips, cut into 1" pieces
1 stalk celery, cut into 1" pieces
1 small turnip, sliced
1 bay leaf
2 cans chicken broth
1 pkg. frozen peas or 1½ cup fresh

*Serves 6 to 8*
*We made dumplings following instructions on box of Bisquick and added 2-3 Tbs. chopped green onions.*

Coat chicken well with flour, salt and pepper. Add oil to Dutch oven and lightly brown chicken in oil. Remove chicken and discard all but 2 or 3 Tbs. drippings. Add onions and cook 6 or 7 minutes, adding garlic for last 2 or 3 minutes. Put chicken, carrots, parsnips, celery, turnip, bay leaf and chicken broth into pot, cover and cook slowly for ½ hour. Remove chicken skin and bones and bay leaf. Return meat to pot; add peas and simmer 10 minutes more. Top with dumplings.

# Cranberry Meatloaf

2 lb. ground chuck
1 large onion, chopped
1½ cups Wheaties
1 egg, beaten
½ green pepper, chopped
2 tsp. salt
½ tsp. parsley flakes
milk to soften mixture
16 oz. jar whole cranberry sauce
2-3 Tbs. light brown sugar

*Preheat oven to 350°*

Combine first eight ingredients. Put in greased loaf pan. Bake at 350° for 1 hour. Mix cranberry sauce and sugar. Cover meatloaf with cranberry mixture and bake for 15 minutes more.

# Lemon Chicken

1 cup fresh lemon juice
4 Tbs. cooking oil
2 Tbs. Dijon mustard
2 Tbs. soy sauce
½ tsp. cayenne pepper
3 lbs. chicken pieces
6 scallions, chopped coarsely

Mix first five ingredients in large bowl. Marinate chicken in mixture for 2-3 hours. Broil, barbecue or bake (350°) for 20-30 minutes. Garnish with lemon wedges and scallions.

# Northern Pike Cakes

2 cups pike fillets, boned, uncooked
1 tsp. Old Bay seafood seasoning
1 egg, beaten
1 cup mashed potatoes
¼ cup butter

Mince raw pike fillets using meat grinder or food processor. Combine fish with seasoning, egg and potatoes and form into cakes. In frying pan lightly saute in hot butter until golden. Remove from pan, place on heated platter and bake at 300° for ½ hour. Serve with mornay sauce.

## Mornay Sauce

¼ cup butter
¼ cup flour
¼ cup water
¾ cup milk
½ cup grated gruyère cheese
¼ cup grated Parmesan cheese

Melt butter, stir in flour to make a roux. Stir over medium heat unitl golden. Slowly add water and milk stirring constantly to blend. Bring to a boil, lower heat, add grated cheeses, heating until cheese melts.

*Boil a pared potato in lard to keep it sweet.*—1889

# Pepper Steak

2 lbs. beef round steak, cut into 1" strips
2 Tbs. corn oil
¼ cup soy sauce
1 cup onion, chopped
2 garlic cloves, minced
½ tsp. salt
¼ tsp. pepper
¼ tsp. ginger
1 can tomatoes with liquid, cut up
2 large green peppers, cut into 1" strips
1½ Tbs. cornstarch
½ cup water

*Make in a 'slow cooker' — Serves 6-8*

Brown steak in oil, then place in slow cooker. Mix next six ingredients and pour over meat. Cook on low heat for 5½-6 hours until tender. Add tomatoes and peppers; cook on low for one more hour. Combine cornstarch and water and stir into liquid in cooker. Cook on high until sauce is thickened. Serve over noodles. If not enough liquid, add a small can of tomato sauce.

*Leave the husks on the corn when you freeze it. This way you'll enjoy fresh-tasting corn on the cob in the winter.*

# Easy Steak Dinner

2 Tbs. butter
1 envelope dry onion soup mix
1½ lbs. cube steak
1 can cream of mushroom soup

*Preheat oven to 375°—Serves 4 to 6*

Place aluminum foil in baking pan and put 1 Tbs. of butter in the center. Sprinkle one half of the soup mix onto the foil. Over this, place steak. Top steak with remaining soup mix and butter. Spread can of mushroom soup over and around steak. Seal foil tightly and bake at 375° for 1-1½ hours.

# Easy Beef Burgundy

3½-4 lbs. beef, cut into 1" pieces
2 cans golden mushroom soup, undiluted
1 cup Burgundy wine
1 pkg. onion soup mix
8-10 fresh mushrooms, sliced

*Leftovers are even better—Serves 8 to 10*

Mix first four ingredients together and marinate overnight. Add mushrooms and cook at 325° for three hours or more. Serve with noodles. If mixture is too thick, a little more wine may be added.

# Grandmom's Meatballs & Spaghetti Sauce

2 lbs. chuck and 1 lb. lean pork butt, ground together
½ - 1 cup fresh Italian parsley, chopped
4 cloves garlic, minced
1 - 3 Tbs. salt
1 cup grated Parmesan cheese
2 - 3 slices Italian bread, broken into crumbs
¼ - ½ cup milk
3 eggs, beaten
¼ cup olive oil, for frying

Mix all ingredients well. Form into balls and fry in hot oil. Add leftover oil to sauce.

## Spaghetti Sauce

1 - 2 Tbs. olive oil
3 - 4 cloves garlic, halved and crushed
2 cans tomato puree
2 cans crushed tomatoes
1 can water
bay leaf
black pepper to taste
½ tsp. sugar
¼ cup grated Parmesan cheese

Saute garlic in oil until golden. Add crushed tomatoes, tomato puree and one can water and bring to a boil. Reduce heat and add bay leaf, pepper, sugar and cheese. Simmer on low heat for 1-2 hours. Better made a day ahead if possible. If sauce becomes too thick, add a little more water.

# Turkey Noodle Bake

½ cup milk
1 can cream of mushroom soup, undiluted
1 cup cooked turkey, chopped
1 cup cheddar cheese, shredded
1 small onion, chopped
8 oz. pkg. medium noodles
1 cup water
¼ cup bread crumbs

*Serves 4 —Preheat oven to 350°*

In 2 qt. casserole stir milk and soup together. Add turkey, cheese and onion. Mix well. Stir in uncooked noodles, coating with soup mixture. Pour water over mixture. Top with bread crumbs. Bake, covered, in a 350° oven 50 minutes or until noodles are tender.

*A cloth wet with turpentine will make shades look new, but they must be dusted before wiping them with this—*c. 1900

# Sauerbraten

2 cups water
½ cup beer
1½ cup red wine vinegar
8 - 10 cloves
4 bay leaves
a few peppercorns
1 carrot, finely chopped
1 stalk celery, finely chopped
3½ - 4 lb. eye of the round roast of beef (or rump roast)
¼ cup margarine

*Serves 8*

Combine all above ingredients except meat and margarine, and bring to a boil. Put meat in a large bowl. Pour marinade over meat, cover and refrigerate 2-3 days, turning twice daily. To cook meat, remove from marinade, pat dry, saving marinade. Brown roast in margarine in Dutch oven. Strain marinade, discarding vegetables and spices, and pour over meat. Cover and simmer for 3-4 hours. When tender remove roast and slice. Keep warm in serving dish or platter. Leave liquid in Dutch oven to make gravy.

## Gravy

1½ cups water
6 Tbs. sugar
1½ cups ginger snap crumbs

Add water and sugar to liquid in Dutch oven. Bring to a boil, reduce heat, add ginger snap crumbs and simmer until gravy thickens, stirring continuously. If too thick, add a little more water. Pour over meat; serve remainder with noodles and sweet and sour cabbage. Also good using venison instead of beef.

# Glazed Pork Roast

6 lb. pork loin
1 tsp. pepper
1 tsp. rosemary
2 tsp. salt
3 cups currant jelly
2 tsp. vinegar
1 tsp. dry mustard
2 Tbs. port wine

*Preheat oven to 350°*

Have roast at room temperature. Place meat, fat side up, in roasting pan. Sprinkle with pepper, rosemary and salt and roast at 350° for 30 minutes per pound or to 185° on meat thermometer. Mix last four ingredients and cook for 10 minutes, stirring often. Pour over meat before serving.

*Try adding a little chopped parsley to the mashed potatoes; it gives them a delicious flavor.*—c. 1900

# Chicken Broccoli Casserole

4 boneless, skinless chicken breast halves, cut into 1" cubes
1 bunch fresh broccoli florets or 16 oz. bag frozen
4½ oz. can sliced mushrooms, drained
½ cup mayonnaise
1 can cream of mushroom soup, undiluted
1 cup cheddar cheese, shredded
bread crumbs

*Serves 6-8 — Preheat oven to 350°*

Put all ingredients into large casserole dish. Stir together and top with bread crumbs. Bake at 350° for ½ hour, until bubbly.

# Potato and Tuna Casserole

2 Tbs. butter or margarine
2 Tbs. onion, minced
3 Tbs. flour
1 tsp. salt
2 cups milk
7 oz. can tuna, drained and flaked
4 cups raw potatoes, thinly sliced

*Serves 4-6 — Preheat oven to 350°*

Melt butter in saucepan and saute onion. Blend in flour and salt. Gradually stir in milk and cook over medium heat until thickened. Stir in tuna. Put potato slices in greased 1-qt. casserole and stir in tuna mixture. Cover and bake in 350° oven for 1 hour. Uncover and continue baking until potatoes are done.

# Cranberry Pork Roast

3 lb. boneless rolled pork loin
16 oz. can jellied cranberry sauce
½ cup sugar
½ cup cranberry juice
1 tsp. dry mustard
¼ tsp. ground cloves
2 Tbs. cornstarch
2 Tbs. cold water
salt to taste

*Made in a 'slow cooker' — Serves 6-8*

Place pork in slow cooker. In a bowl, mash cranberry sauce; stir in sugar, cranberry juice, mustard and cloves. Pour over roast. Cover and cook on low for 6-8 hours. Remove roast and keep warm. To make gravy, skim fat from liquid. Measure 2 cups liquid (add water if necessary) and bring to a boil in saucepan. Combine cornstarch and cold water to make a paste; stir into liquid. Cook and stir until thickened. Season with salt to taste. Serve with sliced pork.

*Tepid water with a little borax dissolved in it is good to wash table linen in.—1889*

# North Country Meat Pie

1½ lb. ground pork
1 small onion, chopped
½ clove garlic or ¼ tsp. garlic powder
½ tsp. salt
½ tsp. dry mustard
½ tsp. thyme
¼ tsp. sage
½ cup water
double pie crust

Simmer above ingredients for 30 minutes in a large skillet. Pour into large pie pan lined with pie crust. Top with second crust, making slits in top. Bake at 375° for 35 minutes or until done.

*To clean aluminum perfectly, rub with cloth wet with coal oil and covered with salt.*—c. 1900

# Overnight Chicken Casserole

8 slices day-old white bread
4 cups cooked chicken, diced
4½ oz. jar sliced mushrooms, drained
8 oz. can sliced water chestnuts, drained
4 eggs
2 cups milk
½ cup mayonnaise
½ tsp. salt
6 to 8 slices (6 oz.) process American cheese
10¾ oz. can condensed cream of celery soup, undiluted
10¾ oz. can condensed cream of mushroom soup, undiluted
2 oz. jar chopped pimentos, drained
1 Tbs. butter, melted

*Serves 8 to 10 — Preheat oven to 325°*

Remove the crusts from bread and set aside. Arrange bread slices in a greased 13x9x2 baking dish. Top with chicken; cover with mushrooms and water chestnuts. Beat eggs; blend in milk, mayonnaise and salt. Pour over chicken. Arrange cheese on top. Combine soups and pimentos pour over cheese. Cover and refrigerate overnight. Before baking, crumble crusts; toss with melted butter. Sprinkle over casserole. Bake, uncovered at 325° for 1¼ hours or until set. Let stand 10 minutes before cutting.

*Soak nuts in salt water overnight before cracking. The nut meats will come out whole instead of in pieces.*

# Michigans

1-2 lbs. hamburg
2 large onion, finely chopped
1 green pepper, finely chopped
1 tsp. salt
½ tsp. pepper, finely chopped
2-3 tsp. chili powder
1 tsp. Italian seasoning
1 tsp. oregano
1 tsp basil
1 tsp. dry mustard
1½ cup water
2  6-oz. cans tomato paste
hot dog buns

Fry hamburg with onion, green pepper and seasonings; drain well. Add water and tomato paste. Simmer 1 hour or longer. Serve over hot dogs in bun. Garnish with finely chopped onions.

*When eggs are scarce and they are needed for puddings, a dessertspoonful of cornstarch may be substituted for one egg.*

# North Country Perch

1 to 1½ cup flour
¼ tsp. rosemary
3-4 lb. perch, skinned and filleted
½ cup olive oil
1 cup water
2-3 Tbs. honey
½ c. lime juice
1 clove garlic, minced
parsley
lime slices

Mix flour and rosemary; coat perch. Heat oil in a heavy skillet and fry perch over medium heat, turning once to brown both sides. Remove fish and drain on paper towels. In small suacepan mix water, honey, lime juice and garlic. Bring to a boil. Return fish to frying pan, add liquid mixture and simmer uncovered for 6-7 minutes. Garnish with parsley and lime slices.

# Batter for Pan Fried Fish

2 cups Bisquick
1 egg
1 pkg. onion soup mix
salt and pepper to taste
milk

Combine the above ingredients, adding enough milk to form a batter. Dip fish in the batter and fry.

# Aunt Hattie's Clam Pie

16 oz. can chopped clams
½ cup clam liquor
½ cup half and half
1 egg, beaten
½ cup cracker crumbs
pastry for two-crust pie
butter or margarine

*Preheat oven to 375°*

Mix first five ingredients together and pour into pastry-lined 9"
pie plate. Dot with butter. Cover with top crust in which you
make slits. Bake at 375° for 1 hour to 1 hour 15 minutes, or until
crust is golden.

# Grilled Lake Trout

1 lake trout
2 lemons, sliced
1 onion, sliced
coursely ground black pepper

Wash and clean trout. Place lemon and onion in body cavity and
sprinkle with pepper to taste. Wrap tightly in foil and place on
a medium grill, turning several times to allow fish to cook
evenly. Cook 30 minutes to 1 hour, depending on size of fish.
Flesh should flake easily when done.

# Salmon Loaf

1 lg. can salmon
1 cup cooked rice
½ can cream of celery soup
1 small onion, chopped
½ cup cracker crumbs
1 stalk celery, chopped
2 eggs, beaten
¼ cup mayonnaise
¼ tsp. black pepper

Mix all ingredients and bake in loaf pan for 1 hour at 375°.

*Natural, homemade dyes for Easter eggs can be made from the following materials: For yellow, put onion skins in cold water and bring to a boil. For blue, boil leaves from half a head of red cabbage. For pink, boil three sliced beets. Add 1 teaspoon of vinegar to each dye: soak eggs in dyes to set the colors.*

# Ted's Chili

2 lbs. ground beef
1-2 Tbs. vegetable oil
2 lg. onions, peeled and diced
2 green peppers, diced
1 cup dry vermouth
2 -3 tsp. whole cumin seeds
32 oz. can plum tomatoes
48 oz. can red kidney beans, well drained
2 cloves garlic, minced
2 Tbs. Worcestershire sauce
2 Tbs. chili powder
dash of Tabasco sauce
½ tsp. cayenne pepper
1 tsp. salt
2 bay leaves

*Serves 6-8*

Brown meat in vegetable oil in a large, heavy Dutch oven. Add onions, green peppers and dry vermouth, stirring occasionally until onions become translucent. Toast cumin seeds in small skillet over medium heat for 5 - 6 minutes, then grind into powder. Add rest of ingredients, stirring until well blended. Bring to a boil. Cover tightly, reduce heat and simmer for 1 to 2 hours. Remove bay leaves. Serve garnished with chopped onions, green peppers, tomatoes and a dollop of sour cream. Best if prepared ahead and reheated.

# EXTRAS

# Salt Pork Gravy

1 lb. salt pork
2 - 4 cups milk
¼ cup maple syrup
3 - 4 Tbs. flour

Wash salt pork and slice. To "freshen" and prepare the salt pork, place in the bottom of a large cast iron frying pan and add milk to cover. Add maple syrup and allow it to come to a boil and then simmer for 10 minutes. Take out the salt pork and discard the liquid. Return the salt pork to the empty frying pan and brown well on both sides, allowing the drippings to accumulate. This takes considerable time and must have your attention the whole while, or it may burn. Remove the salt pork and set it aside. Remove the frying pan from the heat temporarily, and very gradually add the flour to the grease drippings. Return to the heat and brown the flour. Stir constantly as it forms a bubbling roux. The flour should "absorb" the grease and should appear golden brown. Again remove from the heat and very gradually add in milk, about 2 cups to start with (a wire whisk will help). Return to the heat and bring to a boil again, seasoning to taste with salt and pepper, adding more milk if needed.

*In the old days it was essential to "freshen" the salt pork as it was much saltier than what you buy today. The intent was to remove excess salt. It is still necessary to do the freshening part of this recipe or the gravy will look grey rather than golden brown.*

*The actual salt pork was often eaten by children before it ever got to the table. Otherwise it was saved as a treat for the next breakfast, having a quality between bacon and sausage. It was not unusual to serve salt pork gravy when we were having a cooked ham. If this was the case, the freshening liquid could be saved and used to baste the ham as it cooked.*

# Carnarvonshire Coffee Cake

¾ cup margarine
1 cup sugar
3 eggs
1½ tsp. vanilla
½ cup molasses
3 cups flour (do not sift)
2 tsp. baking soda
1½ tsp. baking powder
¼ tsp. salt
16 oz. container sour cream

## Brown Sugar Mixture

¾ cup brown sugar
½ cup walnuts, chopped
1½ tsp. cinnamon

*Can be made ahead and frozen — Preheat oven to 350°*

Place first 5 ingredients in mixing bowl and beat for 2 minutes. The remaining ingredients are to be thoroughly mixed in a separate bowl. Gradually combine the two mixtures to form a uniform batter. Put ½ of batter into greased tube pan and sprinkle with ½ of the brown sugar mixture. Add remaining batter and top with balance of brown sugar mixture. Bake at 350° for 55 to 60 minutes.

# Soda Crackers

2 qts. flour
1 tsp. baking soda
1 cup butter
1 tsp. cream of tartar
milk or water to mix

*This recipe comes from a very old White House cookbook*

Beat above ingredients well. If needed, mix in more flour until quite brittle. Roll and cut into squares. Prick with a fork and bake in a quick oven.

*Sorry, I'm not sure what degree a "quick oven" is. My mother and grandmother only had to open the oven door and pass their hand in the old wood stove oven briefly and they knew immediately if the oven was a "quick oven" or whatever. I didn't inherit, or acquire, their knack for this.*

*Discolored gilt frames can be brightened if rubbed with a sponge dipped in turpentine.*—c. 1900

# Upside Down French Toast

2 Tbs. margarine
¼ cup brown sugar, packed
4 slices canned pineapple, drained
2 eggs
½ cup milk
¼ tsp. salt
4 thick slices of bread

*Preheat oven to 400°*

Melt margarine in 8 or 9" square pan. Sprinkle with brown sugar. Lay pineapple slices over sugar, spacing evenly. In a separate bowl, beat eggs, milk and salt. Soak bread slices in milk mixture and arrange on top of pineapple slices. Pour extra milk mixture over bread. Bake at 400° for 25 minutes or until set and slightly brown. Invert on serving plate.

*A simple dessert is plain boiled rice served with sugar generously mixed with ground cinnamon. Or you might try brown sugar with boiled rice.*—c. 1900

# Grandma Gregory's Pickles

1 gal. white vinegar
1 cup salt
1 cup dry mustard
½ cup sugar
¼ cup whole allspice
100 small early cucumbers

Scrub cucumbers thoroughly and put in small crock with other ingredients. Cover and keep in a cool place for about 2 weeks, stirring 2-3 times a day.

# Chili Sauce

1 peck tomatoes, quartered
6 peppers, finely chopped
6 large onions, finely chopped
1 Tbs. dried hot pepper pods, finely ground
2 cups brown sugar
3 cups cider vinegar
3 Tbs. salt
1 Tbs. black pepper
1 Tbs. allspice
1 tsp. each ground cloves, ginger, cinnamon, nutmeg
1 tsp. celery seed
2 Tbs. dry mustard

Combine above and simmer on stove for about 3 hours. Put in sterile jars.

# Blueberry Fritters

1 cup flour, sifted
1 tsp. baking powder
½ tsp. salt
1 Tbs. sugar
2 egg yolks
¼ cup milk
1 Tbs. corn oil
1½ cups blueberries or chopped fruit
2 egg whites, stiffly beaten
corn oil for frying
light, dark or maple flavored corn syrup

*A "golden oldy" recipe which serves 4-6*

Sift together first four ingredients. Combine egg yolks, milk and corn oil; add to dry ingredients; mix until well blended. Add blueberries (or chopped fruit). Fold in stiffly beaten egg whites. For shallow frying, pour corn oil into skillet to a 1" depth. For deep frying, fill kettle one-third full. Heat oil to 375°. Drop fritters from a tablespoon into hot oil and fry 3 to 4 minutes, turning to brown evenly. Fry only a few fritters at a time. Drain on absorbent paper. If desired, fritters may be pan-fried. Heat about ½ cup corn oil in a skillet. Fry fritters to a golden brown on one side. Turn to brown on other side. Serve warm with corn syrup flavor of your choice, or with the real McCoy—maple syrup.

# Mashed Potato Doughnuts

2 eggs, beaten
2 cups sugar
1 tsp. butter, melted
1 cup milk
4 tsp. baking powder
1 tsp. vanilla
2 cups leftover mashed potatoes
2¾ cups flour (more if needed)
vegetable oil

Mix eggs, sugar, butter, milk, baking powder and vanilla with the mashed potatoes. Add the flour. Roll dough out on floured surface. Cut out with donut cutter and deep fry in hot oil until done, 3-4 minutes. Sprinkle with cinnamon or confectioners' sugar while warm.

# Boom Booms

1 lb. confectioners' sugar
18 oz. jar chunky peanut butter
3 cups Rice Krispies
1 stick butter or margarine, melted
½ stick paraffin
12 oz. bag semi-sweet chocolate chips

Mix sugar, peanut butter, Rice Krispies and butter together thoroughly and form into about sixty 1" balls. Chill in refrigerator for ½ hour. Melt paraffin and chocolate chips in double boiler. Dip balls in hot chocolate, and set on cookie sheet lined with waxed paper. Chill to set. *Note:* Keep chocolate hot in double boiler while dipping.

# Hot Fruit Medley

8¼ oz. can sliced pineapple
20 oz. can peach halves
1 jar apple rings
20 oz. can pear halves
20 oz. can apricot halves
1 stick butter
½ cup brown sugar
flour
1 cup sherry

Drain all fruit. Halve pineapple slices, arrange fruit in layers in medium deep oven-proof dish. Combine butter, sugar, flour and sherry in double boiler, cook, stirring until thickened. Pour over fruit, cover and let stand in refrigerator overnight. Before serving heat in 350° oven until bubbly.

# Plum Conserve

5 lbs. blue Italian plums
5 oranges
5 lbs. sugar
1 lb. raisins
½ lb. walnuts, chopped

Wash plums and cut into quarters, removing pits. Squeeze juice from the oranges and save. Grind the orange peels. Put plums, sugar, ground oranges, orange juice and raisins into a deep pan and simmer for 2 to 3 hours. Stir often. When syrup begins to form, add walnuts. Cook until thickened, approximately ten minutes. Pour into prepared jars. Use paraffin on top of jars and when cooled, add another layer of wax; seal.

# Egg and Sausage Casserole

6 hard boiled eggs, sliced
salt
pepper
1 lb. bulk spicy breakfast sausage
1½ cups sour cream
½ cup dry bread crumbs
1½ cups cheddar cheese, grated

*Serves 6 — Preheat oven to 350°*
*This dish plus Bloody Marys, Hot Fruit Medley, hot rolls,*
*muffins and coffee or tea makes a great company brunch.*

Place eggs in buttered casserole dish. Season with salt and pepper to taste. Brown sausage in skillet, drain and sprinkle over eggs. Pour sour cream over sausage. Mix bread crumbs and grated cheese. Sprinkle over casserole. Bake in 350° oven to heat thoroughly and brown under broiler. Serve piping hot. Except for adding bread crumbs and cheese, rest can be prepared ahead of time.

*To keep suet fresh, chop roughly and sprinkle with a little gran-*
*ulated sugar.*—c. 1900

# Ham & Cheese Strata

16 slices white bread, crusts removed
16 slices ham, thinly sliced
8 slices Old English cheese
8 eggs, beaten
4 cups milk
1 Tbs. onion, finely chopped
½ tsp. dry mustard
½ tsp. salt
2 cups corn flakes, crushed
1 stick butter, melted

*Serves 8 — Preheat oven to 350°*

Make sandwiches with bread, ham and cheese. Arrange in baking dish. Mix eggs, milk, onion, mustard and salt well and pour over sandwiches. Refrigerate overnight. When ready to bake, top with crushed corn flakes and melted butter. Bake at 350° for 1 hour.

*For cleaning oil cloth, saturate a cloth with sweet milk and rub well.—1889*

# Special Macaroni & Cheese

1 cup milk, scalded
2 slices bread, cubed
1 egg, well beaten
1½ cups macaroni, cooked
½ cup extra sharp cheese, diced
½ cup American cheese, diced
1 cup onions, minced
1 Tbs. parsley, minced
3 Tbs. pimentos, minced
3 Tbs. butter, melted
1 tsp. salt
1 tsp. mustard
¼ tsp. pepper

*Serves 6 — Preheat oven to 375°*

Pour milk over bread, add egg and mix well. Add all other ingredients. Pour into large casserole dish. Place dish in pan of
boiling water; bake at 375° for 45 minutes.

*Make good use of clean, discarded stockings to store onions in
the basement. The stocking can be hung up to allow plenty of air
circulation.*

# Red Flannel Hash

2-3 Tbs. butter or margarine
1½ cups potatoes, boiled and diced
1½ cups beets, cooked and diced
1½ cups corn beef, cooked and diced
1 onion, finely chopped
¼ cup half and half
½ tsp. salt
½ tsp. pepper
½ tsp. paprika

Melt butter or margarine in a skillet. Mix all other ingredients thoroughly and pack in skillet. Cook covered over very low heat 30 to 40 minutes or until bottom is crusty.

*A very little lemon or vinegar added to raisins when chopped will prevent them sticking together.*

# VEGETABLES

# Maple Baked Beans

16 oz. (2 cups) dry pea or navy beans
8 cups cold water
6 oz. salt pork, cut in ½" cubes
½ cup onion, chopped
½ cup maple syrup
¼ cup packed brown sugar
1 tsp. salt
1 tsp. dry mustard

*Serves 8—Preheat oven to 300°*

Rinse beans, place in large kettle with water. Bring to boil. Reduce heat; simmer 2 minutes. Remove from heat. Cover; let stand 1 hour. Do not drain. (Or, add beans to water and soak overnight.) Bring beans and soaking water to a boil. Simmer, covered, about 40 minutes, until beans are nearly tender. Drain, reserving liquid. In 2-quart bean pot or casserole combine beans, 1 cup of the reserved cooking liquid, the salt pork, onion, maple syrup, brown sugar, salt and mustard. Cover and bake in 300° oven about 3½ to 4 hours, stirring occasionally. Add a little reserved liquid during baking, if needed.

*Brasswork can be kept bright by occasionally rubbing with salt and vinegar.—c. 1900*

# Garlic Mashed Potatoes

3½-4 lbs. potatoes, peeled and quartered
8 large garlic cloves, peeled
2 Tbs. butter
1 Tbs. fresh or 2 tsp. dried rosemary
1-1½ cups chicken broth
½ cup grated Parmesan cheese
salt and pepper to taste

*We often make this an hour or two ahead and put it in a casserole dish and reheat in 350° oven for 30-35 minutes, adding more broth if too dry.*

Cook potatoes and peeled garlic in salted water until soft. Drain. In large bowl or pan, using an electric mixer, beat potatoes and garlic. Add butter and rosemary; beat until smooth. Heat cup of broth to just boiling and mix into potatoes. Add Parmesan cheese and mix well. Salt and pepper to taste. Garnish with fresh rosemary, if available, or sprinkle with paprika.

*To make gravy with less grease, pour off the drippings from a roast or poultry and add a couple ice cubes. The grease will stick to the cubes, and you can lift them out.*

# Apple Potato Delight

4 large potatoes, peeled and cut into pieces
4 tart apples, peeled, cored and cut into quarters
salt
sugar to taste
¼ tsp. nutmeg
4 Tbs. butter, room temperature

*A German dish excellent with pork, grilled sausages and spareribs — Serves 4-6*

Cook potatoes in enough water to cover for about 10 minutes or until they are about three-quarters soft. Drain off about half the water. Add the apples; mix and cook until they are tender. Mash the mixture and season with salt and sugar to taste. Stir in nutmeg and the butter and beat until light.

# Glazed Onions

16 medium onions
¼ cup catsup
½ to ¾ cup honey
½ cup butter or margarine, melted

*Preheat oven to 350°*

Boil onions until partly cooked. Mix catsup, honey and butter and pour over onions in a casserole dish. Bake at 350°, basting often, until onions are tender.

# Eggplant Parmesan

1 cup tomato puree
1 cup water
¼ tsp. baking soda
2 cups oil
2 eggplants, about 2-2½ lbs., peeled and cut into 1/8" slices
1 cup flour
6 extra large eggs, beaten
grated Parmesan cheese
salt to taste

*Preheat oven to 350°*

Prepare sauce in advance. Combine tomato puree and water in saucepan. Cook for 30 minutes, adding baking soda as it cooks. Heat oil in heavy skillet. Dip each eggplant slice in flour and then in beaten eggs. Brown quickly in hot oil. Pour tomato sauce into bottom of 2-qt. casserole to just cover bottom, sprinkle with Parmesan cheese. Layer eggplant, sauce and cheese. Bake uncovered at 350° for 30 minutes.

*Drop a lettuce leaf into the soup pot to absorb excess grease. Simply remove the saturated leaf before serving.*

# Summer Squash Casserole

2 cups cooked zucchini or other squash, cut into ¾" slices
1 can cream of chicken soup
½ cup sour cream
grated Parmesan cheese
buttered bread crumbs

*Preheat oven to 350°*

Cook 2 cups squash until tender. Drain; set aside. In a separate bowl, mix condensed soup and sour cream together. Put ½ squash in bottom of buttered casserole. Cover with ½ soup mixture. Add second layer. Sprinkle with Parmesan cheese and cover with buttered bread crumbs. Bake in 350° oven for 15-20 minutes. Place under broiler for 2-3 minutes to brown.

# Spinach Casserole

2 pkg. frozen chopped spinach
1 cup sour cream
¼ tsp. marjoram
¼ tsp. pepper
3 slices bacon, fried crisp and crumbled
½ cup cheddar cheese, shredded

*Preheat oven to 325°*

Cook and drain spinach. Place in greased casserole dish. Pour sour cream over spinach, sprinkle with marjoram and pepper. Bake for 15 minutes at 325°. Sprinkle bacon and cheese over top and bake another 5-10 minutes until cheese melts and bubbles.

# Cheese Potatoes

lg. pkg. frozen hash brown potatoes
1 medium onion, chopped
4 Tbs. margarine
1 can cream of chicken soup
1½ cups cheddar cheese, shredded
8 oz. carton sour cream
bread crumbs

*Preheat oven to 350°*

Break up potatoes and spread in buttered baking dish. Sprinkle with onion. Melt margarine, add soup and cheese; heat until cheese is melted. Remove from heat, stir in sour cream and pour over potatoes. Sprinkle with bread crumbs. Bake at 350° for 45-50 minutes.

# Potato Scallop

6 large potatoes, thinly sliced
1 large onion, thinly sliced
2 Tbs. butter or margarine
2 Tbs. flour
1 cup milk
salt and pepper to taste

*Preheat oven to 325°*

Alternate layers of potatoes and onions in greased 9 x 13 baking dish. Make white sauce of last four ingredients. Cover with white sauce; dot with butter. Bake at 325° for 1 hour or more.

# Broccoli Casserole

¼ cup onion, chopped
4 Tbs. margarine
1 can cream of chicken soup
¼ soup can of milk
½ cup rice, cooked
3 pkgs. chopped broccoli, cooked and drained
1 small jar Cheez Whiz
paprika

*Preheat oven to 350°*

Brown onion in margarine and add soup and milk. Cool cooked rice and broccoli 10 minutes and drain. Add rice, broccoli and Cheez Whiz to soup mixture and pour into casserole. Bake at 350° for 20-25 minutes until bubbly. Sprinkle paprika on top.

# Cheese and Carrot Casserole

2 cups carrots, cooked and mashed
3 eggs, well beaten
2 cups grated cheddar cheese
1 small onion, grated
½ tsp. salt
¼ tsp. pepper
paprika

*Preheat oven to 325°*

Mix first six ingredients together and pour into greased casserole dish. Sprinkle with paprika. Bake at 325° for 40 minutes.

# Baked Apple and Onion

apples, peeled and sliced
onions, sliced
brown sugar
salt
butter
bread crumbs

*Serves as many as you need depending on size of dish.*

Grease casserole dish. Arrange in layers sliced apples, sliced onions, 2 or 3 Tbs. brown sugar and a sprinkle of salt. Repeat layers until dish is heaping (it will settle as it cooks). Top with bread crumbs and several small bits of butter. Bake, covered, at 300° for approximately 2 hours; uncover for last ½ hour to brown crumbs. Serve piping hot.

# Sautéed Cucumbers

1 lb. cucumbers, peeled and cut into 2" slices
1 tsp. salt
2 Tbs. butter
1 Tbs. fresh dill, finely chopped
black pepper to taste

Place cucumbers in a bowl and sprinkle with salt. Let sit for 30 minutes, then pat dry. Sauté cucumbers in butter over medium heat for 4-6 minutes. Sprinkle with dill and season with pepper. Serve hot.

# DESSERTS

# Maple Rhubarb Crumble

5 cups rhubarb, cut into ½" slices
¼ cup maple syrup
1 tsp. lemon peel, grated
3 Tbs. butter
¼ cup regular oatmeal
¼ cup flour
¼ cup brown sugar, tightly packed

*Delicious with vanilla ice cream — Preheat oven to 350°*

Combine rhubarb, syrup and lemon peel; put into greased 8-inch baking dish. Melt butter and add oatmeal, flour and brown sugar and mix thoroughly; sprinkle over rhubarb mixture. Bake at 350° for 50 minutes or until rhubarb is tender.

*When mixing pie crust or baking powder biscuits, they will be much lighter if a fork is used.*—c. 1900

# Never-Fail Chocolate Cake

1 egg
½ cup cocoa
½ cup shortening
1½ cups flour
½ cup buttermilk or sour milk
1 tsp. vanilla
1 tsp. baking soda
¼ tsp. salt
1 cup sugar
½ cup boiling water

*Preheat oven to 350°*

Put ingredients in bowl in order given above. Beat together and pour into a 9 x 13-inch greased and floured pan. Bake at 350° for 25-30 minutes.

*Bob's mother, Caroline Igoe, who taught him to cook was a wonderful baker. This was one of her favorite recipes.*

# Maple Syrup Apple Crunch

1 qt. apples, peeled and sliced
1 cup maple syrup
cinnamon
1 cup sifted flour
½ cup dark brown sugar
1 tsp. salt
½ cup margarine

*Serves 6 — Preheat oven to 350°*

Put apples in greased 6 x 10-inch baking dish. Pour the maple syrup over the apples and sprinkle on some cinnamon. Blend flour, salt and cut in margarine to make a crumbly mixture. Spread this evenly over the apples and syrup. Bake at 350° for 50 minutes. Serve piping hot with whipped cream or vanilla ice cream.

*The original recipe called for ¾ cup of light brown sugar and ¼ cup water instead of the maple syrup. Lacking the light brown sugar, we used syrup instead and found it a delightful substitute.*

# Corn Flake Macaroons

2 egg whites, beaten until light
1 cup sugar
1 cup shredded coconut
1 tsp. vanilla
3 cups corn flakes

*Preheat oven to 350°*

Mix all ingredients together and blend well. Drop in spoonfuls on buttered baking sheet, keeping well separated. Bake at 350° for 10 to 11 minutes. Do not overbake.

# Ginger Drops

1 cup light brown sugar
¾ cup butter or margarine
½ cup cold water
1 egg
¾ cup molasses
2 rounded Tbs. ginger
1 rounded tsp. soda
3½ cups flour

*Makes 35 to 40 — Preheat oven to 350°*

Mix all ingredients together; will make thick dough. Drop from teaspoon onto well greased or non-stick cookie sheet. Bake at 350° for 12-15 minutes.

# Old Fashioned Blackberry Cobbler

3 Tbs. quick-cooking tapioca
1 cup sugar
¼ tsp. salt
¼ tsp. cinnamon
4 cups blackberries
1 cup water
1 Tbs. lemon juice
1 Tbs. butter or margarine
1 cup biscuit mix
2 Tbs. sugar
light cream
1 tsp. cinnamon

*Serves 8 — Preheat oven to 375°*

Mix first six ingredients together in a saucepan. Cook and stir over moderate heat until mixture comes to a boil. Remove from heat; add lemon juice and butter. Pour into a 12 x 7-inch baking dish and keep warm. Mix biscuit mix with 1 Tbs. sugar; add cream and stir until soft dough is formed. Turn onto a lightly floured board or prepared pastry cloth and knead ten times. Pat lightly to about ¼" thickness. Cut out eight 2" biscuits. Place biscuits on top of blackberry mixture. Then mix 1 Tbs. sugar and 1 tsp. cinnamon and sprinkle over biscuits. Bake in 375° oven for 30 minutes or until biscuits are baked through. Serve warm with cream.

# Rhubarb Cobbler

¾ cup butter
¾ cup flour
¼ cup sugar
1 tsp. baking powder
½ cup milk
2 cups rhubarb, chopped
1 cup sugar
¼ tsp. baking soda

Melt butter and pour into baking dish. Mix next four ingredients and pour over butter in baking dish. Mix rhubarb, 1 cup sugar and baking soda together and spoon over batter. Bake at 350° for 45-60 minutes.

*A scant cup of butter will often make a cake lighter than a full one.*—1889

# Applesauce Cake

2½ cups unsweetened applesauce
½ cup butter
2 cup sugar
1 tsp. cinnamon
1 tsp. allspice
1 tsp. ground cloves
¼ tsp. salt
1 tsp. baking soda
3 cups flour
1 cup raisins (optional)
1 cup walnuts, chopped (optional)

*Preheat oven to 325°*

Warm applesauce in a saucepan. Cream butter and sugar. Combine all ingredients and mix well. Pour into greased 9 x 13-inch baking pan. Bake at 325° for 35-40 minutes.

*To keep your homemade ice cream from melting too quickly, add one tablespoon unflavored gelatin dissolved in a quarter-cup of hot water to the milk mixture before freezing.*

# Maple Syrup Pie

1½ Tbs. butter
2 Tbs. flour
2 egg yolks
1 cup maple syrup
½ cup water
1 cup butternuts, chopped
1 baked pie shell
whipped cream

*This pie is similar to pecan pie, in fact, sadly enough, pecans or walnuts can be substituted for the butternut meats. At its best, the maple syrup should be "heavy," meaning boiled down more than usual, such that some maple sugar crystals line the inside of the container in which it was stored.*

Cream butter and flour together. Add egg yolks, maple syrup and water. Cook in a double boiler until thick. Add nut meats. Pour into baked pie shell and cover with whipped cream when cool. If whipped cream is added as the pie is served, the pie can be served while still warm, and many think it best that way.

*Butternuts have a heavy sticky outer husk when first picked. If you are very patient, you can "age" this away by spreading them out to dry for a few months before trying to shell any of them. The green outer husk will dehydrate and become black. In this condition the husk is more eaily removed by scuffing the nuts between your shoe and a concrete floor.*

# Pumpkin Fool

2 cups heavy cream
2 Tbs. confectioners' sugar
1 tsp. vanilla
30 oz. can pumpkin pie filling
1 tsp. ground cinnamon
½ tsp. ground nutmeg
1 square semi-sweet chocolate, grated

*Serves 8*

In small bowl, with mixer at medium speed, beat cream, confectioners' sugar and vanilla until stiff. In large bowl, mix pumpkin pie filling, cinnamon and nutmeg. Fold whipped cream into pumpkin mixture to created a marbled effect. Spoon mixture into eight wine glasses or dessert bowls; sprinkle with chocolate. Refrigerate until ready to serve.

*When cleaning pumpkins or winter squash, use a grapefruit spoon to easily remove the seeds.*

# Apple Pie

Crust for 2-crust pie
1 cup sugar
1 Tbs. flour
3-4 cups apples, peeled and thinly sliced
½ cup sharp American cheese, crumbled
½ stick chilled margarine or butter
cinnamon

Line pie plate with crust. Mix sugar and flour and shake 3-4 Tbs. over bottom crust. Fill pie plate half full of apples. Sprinkle half of remaining sugar mixture over apples and half of the cheese. Fill dish with remaining apples and sprinkle the rest of sugar mixture, cheese, margarine and some cinnamon over the apples. Add top crust, wrapping edges over bottom crust, pressing with fork to seal. Make 8-10 slits in top crust. Bake at 400° for about an hour.

# Ellie's Pie Crust

2 cups flour (do not sift)
¾ tsp. salt
1 cup less 1 Tbs. butter flavored Crisco
¼ cup cold milk

*We've had Ellie's pies and they're wonderful*

Mix salt and flour. Cut shortening into flour mixture until size of a pea. Stir in cold milk and mix with a fork. Work dough with hands into a soft ball. Divide in half and roll out onto lightly on floured board. Will make a double crust pie or two shells.

# Pineapple Pie

Crust for 2-crust pie
4 cups crushed pineapple
4 Tbs. cornstarch
½ tsp. salt
1 cup sugar
2 Tbs. butter
1 Tbs. lemon juice

*A favorite at the I-Go-Inn back in the 1930's and '40's*

Cook pineapple, cornstarch, salt and sugar until mixture thickens. stirring constantly. Remove from heat. Add butter and lemon juice, stir thoroughly. Pour into unbaked pie shell. Cover with top crust. Slit crust in several places. Bake at 400° for 35-40 minutes.

*Sweeten your pie crust—adding one tablespoonful of sugar to a pie gives a fine flavor and keeps it fresh.*—c. 1900

# Pumpkin Cake

3 cups flour
1¾ cups sugar
2 tsp. baking soda
2 tsp. baking powder
1 tsp. salt
¾ tsp. cinnamon
4 eggs
2 cups pumpkin pie filling
1 cup vegetable oil
1 cup walnuts, chopped
1 cup chocolate chips

*Preheat oven to 350°*

Sift the dry ingredients together. Add all the liquid ingredients, then add nuts and chocolate chips. Stir until blended. Pour batter into a greased and floured tube pan. Bake at 350° for 1 hour.

*When fresh peaches are ripe, freeze them (without washing) in plastic freezer bags. When ready to use them, take out as many as you need, run hot water over them to remove the skin, and slice.*

# Ruth Macy's Chocolate Cookies

1 cup light brown sugar
½ cup margarine
2 squares semi-sweet chocolate, melted
1 egg
½ cup milk
1½ cups flour
½ tsp. baking soda
½ cup walnuts, chopped

*Preheat oven to 375°*

Cream sugar and margarine. Add all other ingredients and mix together thoroughly. Drop from teaspoon onto greased cookie sheet. Bake at 375° for about 10 minutes. Frost with chocolate or white frosting.

*To soften brown sugar, place a slice of soft bread or a slice of apple in the container and seal tightly. It will be soft in a few hours.*

# Maple Syrup Cake

½ cup sugar
5½ Tbs. shortening
¾ cup maple syrup
½ cup milk
salt
3 tsp. baking powder
2¼ cups flour
3 egg whites, beaten

*Preheat oven to 350°*

Cream the sugar and shortening together. Add the syrup and stir well. Add the milk, baking powder and flour alternately. Fold in the egg whites and bake in an oblong pan at 350-375° for 45-60 minutes. When cake is baked and cooled, frost with Maple Sugar Frosting.

## Maple Sugar Frosting

¾ cup maple syrup
¼ cup sugar
1 egg white, beaten

Cook the syrup and sugar together until it spins a thread (220°) when dropped from a spoon. Pour slowly over the beaten egg white and beat until cold. This icing is quickly made and may be used to give a maple flavor to simple cakes or cookies.

# Cottage Pudding

1¾ cups flour, sifted
2½ tsp. baking powder
½ tsp. salt
¼ cup shortening
1 cup sugar
1 egg
1 tsp. vanilla
¾ cup milk

*An old recipe—a favorite growing up — Serves 6*

Sift flour, baking powder and salt together; set aside. Cream shortening and add sugar gradually. Beat in egg and vanilla. Alternately add flour and milk to sugar mixture, beating after each addition until smooth. Pour into 8x8x2" greased pan, bake at 350° for 30 to 45 minutes. Serve with Nutmeg Sauce.

*The above recipe can be changed to Blueberry Pudding by adding 1 cup of blueberries and can be baked in muffin pans.*

## Nutmeg Sauce

1 cup sugar
1 Tbs. flour
¼ tsp. salt
2 cups boiling water
1 Tbs. butter
1 tsp. nutmeg, grated

Mix the sugar, flour and a pinch of salt well. Add boiling water gradually, stirring continually. Then add the butter and cook for 5 minutes. Remove from heat and stir in nutmeg. Serve hot on Cottage Pudding or Fruit Cobbler.

# Blueberry Sauce

¾ cup sugar
¼ cup cornstarch
dash of nutmeg
1½ cups boiling water
¼ cup butter
½ cup fresh blueberries, crushed
½ cup whole blueberries
¼ cup rum

*Great on ice cream, Cottage Pudding or Blueberry Pudding.*

Mix sugar, cornstarch and nutmeg in a saucepan and gradually stir in boiling water. Bring to a boil, stirring constantly. When mixture thickens, add butter and blueberries. Just before serving, add rum.

*When making a berry pie, spinkle the bottom crust lightly with sugar and flour mixed in equal proportions to keep the bottom crust from becoming soggy.*

# Gingerbread

1 cup butter
2 cups sugar
4 eggs, slightly beaten
1 cup molasses
3 cups flour
1½ Tbs. ginger
1 tsp. baking soda
1 cup sour milk or buttermilk
heavy cream for whipping
confectioners' sugar

*Serves 12 — Preheat oven to 350°*

Beat butter and sugar together until fluffy. Add eggs and molasses. Stir well. Sift flour, ginger and baking soda together. Add to bowl alternately with sour milk or buttermilk, mixing thoroughly. Pour batter into a greased and floured 9 x 13" baking dish. Bake at 350° for 50-60 minutes. Serve warm with whipped cream sweetened with confectioners' sugar.

*Buttering the knife before cutting a meringue pie will produce a clean cut without damaging the meringue.*

# Apple Snow

2 cups unsweetened applesauce
¼ tsp. salt
¼ tsp. nutmeg
1 tsp. vanilla
2 egg whites
¼ cup sugar

To the applesauce add salt, nutmeg and vanilla. Beat egg whites until stiff, gradually sweetening with sugar. Gently fold into applesauce. Chill and serve with cream or whipped cream.

# Indian Pudding

1 qt. milk
¼ cup cornmeal
½ cup molasses
1 tsp. salt
¼ cup light brown sugar
1 Tbs. butter
1 tsp. cinnamon
1 tsp. nutmeg
½ tsp. ginger

Scald milk and stir in cornmeal, cooking slowly about 20 minutes. Add all other ingredients. Mix thoroughly and pour into greased casserole. Bake uncovered at 275° for 3 hours. Serve warm with vanilla ice cream.

# Pumpkin Streusel Squares

1¾ cups flour
½ cup brown sugar
¼ cup sugar
1 cup cold margarine
1 cup walnuts, chopped
16 oz. can pumpkin pie filling
1 can condensed milk
2 eggs
1 tsp. cinnamon

*Makes 12 to 15 — Preheat oven to 350°*

Combine flour and sugars; cut in margarine until crumbly. Stir in walnuts. Set aside 1 cup of mixture. Press remainder into a 12 x 7" baking dish on bottom and half way up sides. In another bowl mix pumpkin pie filling, condensed milk, eggs and cinnamon well and pour into prepared dish. Top with reserved crumb mixture. Bake 55 minutes or until golden. Let cool before cutting into squares.

*A few drops of lemon juice added to whipping cream helps it whip faster and better.*

# Blueberry Cobbler

1 qt. blueberries
1 cup sugar
¼ cup butter, melted
juice of ½ lemon
1 cup cake flour
¼ tsp. nutmeg
3 tsp. baking powder
¼ tsp. salt
3 Tbs. lard
1 egg, beaten
¼ cup milk

*Serves 6 — Preheat oven to 350°*

Put blueberries, sugar, butter and lemon juice in a baking dish. Mix and sift dry ingredients and cut in lard. Beat egg and milk together, then stir in dry ingredients. Cover the blueberries with this mixture. Bake at 350° for 40 minutes. Cut in squares and serve with liberal amount of pudding sauce.

## Pudding Sauce

¼ lb. butter
1 cup sugar
1 tsp. grated nutmeg
1 Tbs. vanilla
2 eggs, well beaten
¼ cup rum or brandy

Cream butter and sugar, then add grated nutmeg and vanilla. Cook in top of double boiler for 5 minutes, then add beaten eggs and flavor with rum or brandy.

# Grandma's Christmas Cookies

4¼ cups all-purpose flour
2 tsp. baking soda
1 cup butter, softened
1 cup brown sugar, firmly packed
2 large eggs
½ cup pure maple syrup
1 tsp. vanilla

*A very old recipe—makes 10 dozen — Preheat oven to 350°*

Combine flour and baking soda in a bowl. Beat butter and sugar until light and fluffy. Beat in eggs, maple syrup and vanilla. Stir in dry ingredients until blended. (Dough will be soft.) Divide into quarters. Roll each quarter ¼" thick between two sheets of wax paper. Stack on a cookie sheet, cover and refrigerate overnight. When ready to bake, peel off wax paper, invert onto floured surface. Cut dough with 2" cookie cutters. Transfer to an ungreased cookie sheet. Bake at 350° for 6 to 8 minutes, until golden. Repeat with remaining dough. Decorate as desired.

# Decorative Icing

1 box (1 lb.) confectioners' sugar
½ tsp. cream of tartar
3 large egg whites
assorted paste food colorings

Combine all ingredients. Beat at medium speed until smooth and at high speed for 5 minutes. Tint icing with food colorings. Store in tightly covered container up to 3 days. Thin with a little water if necessary. Makes 2¾ cups.

# Grandpa's Christmas Cake

2 cups flour
1 tsp. cinnamon
½ tsp. salt
½ tsp. cloves
½ tsp. nutmeg
1 cup raisins
1 cup citrus fruit, chopped
1 cup walnuts, chopped
½ cup melted butter
1 cup sugar
2 tsp. baking soda
1½ cups hot applesauce
rum

*Makes 2 small loaves — Preheat oven to 350°*

Sift first five ingredients together. Add raisins, citrus fruit and walnuts. Mix well. Cream butter and sugar together. Mix with dry ingredients. Add baking soda to applesauce. Mix well with other ingredients. Grease one large or two small loaf pans. Bake 50-60 minutes in 350° oven. When cool removed from pans. Brush loaves with rum. Wrap in plastic wrap and then foil to keep moist.

*You'll get more juice from a lemon if you first warm it in a pan of hot water.*

# Standard Kitchen Measurements

1 cup = 8 fluid oz.
2 cups = 1 pint
4 cups = 1 quart
4 quarts = 1 gallon
2 cups butter = 1 pound
4 cups flour = 1 pound

2 cups gran. sugar = 1 pound
3 teaspoons = 1 tablespoon
4 tablespoons = ¼ cup
2 tablespoons = 1 oz.
16 tablespoons = 1 cup
16 oz. = 1 pound

# Substitutions

| INGREDIENT | SUBSTITUTION |
|---|---|
| 1 tsp. baking powder | ¼ tsp. baking soda plus ½ tsp. cream of tartar |
| 1 c. buttermilk or sour milk | 1 Tbs. white vinegar or lemon juice stirred into 1 c. milk - let stand 5 minutes |
| 1 sq. (1 oz.) unsweetened chocolate | 3 Tbs. unsweetened cocoa plus 1 Tbs. melted butter or margarine |
| juice of 1 lemon | 2 Tbs. bottled lemon juice |
| 1 tsp. dry mustard | 1 Tbs. prepared mustard |

# Index

## Main Courses

## Extras